# Kids Will Be Kids

*Including the Parental Aptitude Test*

# Kids Will Be Kids

## EXCELLENT, TRIED-AND-TRUE REASONS FOR THINKING TWICE ABOUT HAVING CHILDREN

*(or Why You Might Want to Rent Them Out on Weekends)*

## JANE NALIBOFF

**CUMBERLAND HOUSE**

Nashville, Tennessee

Published by Cumberland House Publishing, Inc., 2200 Abbott Martin Road, Suite 102, Nashville, Tennessee 37215.

Distributed to the trade by Andrews and McMeel, 4520 Main Street, Kansas City, Missouri 64111-7701.

Design by Gore Studio, Inc.
Art by Bill Ross

Library of Congress Cataloging-In-Publication Data

Naliboff, Jane, 1951–
   Kids will be kids / Jane Naliboff.
      p.   cm.
   ISBN: 1-888952-31-8 (pbk. : alk. paper)
   1. Parenting—Humor. 2. Children—Humor.   I. Title
PN6231.P2N35  1997
818' .5407—dc21
                           96-54257
                            CIP

Printed in the United States of America
1  2  3  4  5  6  7  8 — 02  01  00  99  98  97

**For Jay,**

my best friend,
who supported me through this
and who always gets my jokes

and

**Courtney, Lauren, and Dana,**

my pearls and inspiration

# Introduction

I am one of those people who has always known, for as long as I can remember, that at some point in my life I would have children. For some reason, however, I always pictured them as babies. Babies sleeping peacefully in my arms, sweet smelling and beautiful. I had no younger siblings while I was growing up, and I really didn't know what it was like to have young children and then teenagers in the house. Of course, I was a child and a teenager all in my own time, but who ever notices what you yourself are? And who ever understands why parents are so tired and cranky all the time? Now I know.

What you are about to read are 600 reasons for why you might want to think twice before having children or, if you already have them—maybe you should have read this first—for at least renting them out.

No one ever told me, for instance, that some children don't sleep through the night until they are three, which means that if you have a second child while number one is two, you will have one year of getting up six times a night, seven days a week, like I did. And that's a normal week, not counting the weeks of stomach flu, chicken pox, pneumonia, strep throat, ear infections, nightmares, and loneliness.

No one ever told me, either, that my precious daughter could lose all her books on the second day of seventh grade, miss the bus home every day for a week, and then let her entire lunch fall out of her lunch bag on the bus—along with her homework. Which she walked off and left.

By the time you finish reading this book, you will realize that it could only have been written by a parent—probably a parent of more than one child. (Actually, I am the mother of three daughters, two dogs, two fish, and three cats—and a husband. Now there's the subject for another book!) As a parent, I have spent more sleepless nights than I ever thought I would, cleaned up more vomit than I care to recall, and looked in more ears, down more throats, and at more skin blemishes than I would have dreamed possible. I have done endless loads of laundry and dishes, cooked an incredible number of meals (that at least one family member hated), and driven millions of miles to lessons, rehearsals, and the orthodontist. I have learned to live with a permanent car seat in my car and sippy cups of one sort or another in my drawers for fifteen years. I do have a degree in psychology, however, which helps. I'm very good at behavior modification. I also happen to be married to a physician, which helps even more, as vomit doesn't make him gag.

But—having made all these disclaimers—even if I had been told in advance all that I have learned about children, I still would have had mine and adored them every day while I walked into walls, vacuumed up glitter, removed glue from my keyboard, tried to find time to work, and slept standing up.

After all, Kids Will Be Kids. What else would we expect?

# Parental Aptitude Test:

Before you decide to go ahead and have kids, or if you already have them, you can take this test designed to tell you if you're cut out to be a parent. If you find that you're not, and you already went ahead and had some, well, you can always rent them out to your neighbors, who probably won't be any better at it than you. Score yourself when you're finished. You'll find easy-to-read comprehensive results on the last page of this book.

Circle the answer that most applies to you. Circle only one answer. Don't cheat.

**1.** You require:
   a. ten hours of sleep a night
   b. eight hours of sleep a night and a good nap in the afternoon
   c. six hours of sleep, if you're allowed to be cranky
   d. three nonconsecutive hours of sleep a night, and you can get by on this for at least six years

**2.** The sight or smell of vomit makes you:
   a. throw up on sight
   b. call your spouse out of an important meeting to come home and clean it up
   c. leave it and run the other way
   d. want to clean it up right away without even holding your breath

**3.** Your idea of a quiet Sunday involves:
   a. reading the paper and watching a football game on television
   b. playing softball with your friends
   c. sleeping until noon and eating brunch out
   d. getting up at the crack of dawn, cooking and cleaning all day and doing a school project on bat caves due on Monday

4. If you saw a two-year-old with green stuff running out of its
      nose, you would:
   a. throw up
   b. tell him/her to wipe it on his/her sleeve
   c. ask him/her if he/she needs a tissue
   d. wipe it for him/her without saying anything (and then gag)

5. When you spend hours cooking dinner you expect:
   a. praise
   b. everyone to eat it
   c. at least someone to like it
   d. the possibility that it could be fed to the dog under the table

6. When you go into the bathroom, you like to:
   a. lock the door and be alone
   b. find it neat and clean the way you left it
   c. not have anyone watch you go
   d. have lots of company, be asked a lot of questions, and have
      to clear a space to sit down

7. You think garbage disposals are for:
    a. grinding up garbage
    b. grinding up bodies in murder mysteries
    c. getting rid of leftovers
    d. making really cool noises when they grind up plastic cars,
       spoons, and aluminum foil

8. In school you took:
    a. car shop
    b. industrial arts
    c. opera
    d. algebra I, algebra II, calculus

9. The floors in your house have:
    a. white wool carpeting
    b. pale green nylon carpeting
    c. brand-new no-wax floors
    d. brown and black indoor outdoor carpeting with lint-hiding
       beige threads running through it

10. All of your clothes:
   a. have to be dry-cleaned
   b. cost over two hundred dollars each
   c. do not allow you to sit on the floor
   d. are poop and spit-up resistant

11. When you buy a new car:
   a. you don't allow anyone to eat in it
   b. only coffee is allowed to be drunk in it
   c. you have a no-sand, no-dirt, no-paper, and no-sticky-stuff rule
   d. you don't mind if it looks like the dump your old car did
      after eight hours

12. When you're talking on the phone:
   a. you want total silence
   b. you tolerate quiet music
   c. you are able to make dinner
   d. you can talk to five other people at the same time while
      cooking dinner, holding a wiggly person, and cleaning up cat
      barf before the dog gets to it

13. When traveling, you:
    a. take only one bag with you
    b. never eat until you reach your destination
    c. try not to use public restrooms
    d. pack as much junk food, juice, games, and books as you can into one of your five bags, which you have to juggle while you check out every public bathroom

14. Dinner time means:
    a. a tablecloth, wine and candles
    b. forty-five minutes of peace with your spouse
    c. a quick dinner and a movie
    d. a fast-paced food arena otherwise known as survival of the fittest, resulting in sweeping and vacuuming

15. When it comes to holiday decorations, you:
    a. like that all-white Victorian look
    b. only buy from antique stores
    c. hate holiday decorations, and holidays for that matter
    d. think construction paper is the way to go, especially orange paper pumpkins and green-and-red paper chains

16. You're so truthful that:
   a. you'd tell all the children waiting in line to see Santa that there's one just like him next door and that his beard is fake
   b. you'd tell Picasso his paintings were no good because they don't look real enough
   c. you'd tell a friend if his clothes didn't match
   d. you'd never say there wasn't a tooth fairy because everyone knows there is

17. When you drive, you:
   a. demand silence
   b. like to listen to classical music and the news only
   c. never let anyone change the radio station
   d. like to sing oldies out loud while eating the middles out of Oreos

Now turn to the last page in this book for the results.

# Kids Will Be Kids

1. You like to sleep.

2. You like sleeping with your spouse.

3. You enjoy quiet time.

4. You like to sleep late on weekends.

5. You want to receive sympathy, not give it.

**6.** You hate knock-knock jokes.

**7.** You hate the same knock-knock jokes day after day.

**8.** You hate doing other people's zippers.

**9.** You hate doing other people's laces.

**10.** You really hate redoing zippers and laces because the person has to pee when you were all done.

**11.** You like to lick the batter bowl yourself.

**12.** You like to lick the beaters yourself.

**13.** You don't want anyone to know that you eat the sugar when you bake.

**14.** You hate macaroni and cheese seven nights a week.

**15.** You hate to do laundry, wash dishes, and cook.

**16.** You like a clean bathroom.

**17.** You don't like company in the bathroom.

**18.** You think toothpaste covers should be replaced each time they're opened.

**19.** You think the sink should be rinsed out after spitting in it.

**20.** You're not good at unclogging the toilet.

**21.** The very thought of reading to someone who is learning to poop in a potty is enough to make you ill.

**22.** You can't stand it when your toothbrush falls in the toilet, accidentally.

**23.** Retrieving hairbrushes, pens, cars, wash-cloths, and your toothbrush from the toilet ruins your day.

**24.** The idea of a ten-year-old sharing your deodorant makes your stomach turn.

**25.** The thought of someone using your makeup could cause you to commit a crime.

**26.** You hate being slimed with jelly.

**27.** You hate peanut butter.

**28.** You hate marshmallow fluff.

**29.** You hate scraping all of the above off of the cabinets and the refrigerator.

**30.** You hate finding all of the above on the toilet seat.

**31.** You want the phone when you want the phone.

**32.** You don't know anything about ear infections, or the scream that goes with them.

**33.** You get defensive if someone doesn't like your cooking.

**34.** You don't like to make more than one thing for dinner.

**35.** You love casseroles.

**36.** You hate creepy crawlies.

**37.** You hate to go to the lake, to the out-house, to the lake, to the outhouse.

**38.** You never liked lacing other people's skates.

**39.** You hate bending over.

**40.** "Mommy" could never be your name.

**41.** You really hate watching small people pee.

**42.** You'd spew if you had to wipe a hiney other than your own.

**43.** The thought of cleaning up vomit makes you want to hurl.

**44.** You absolutely hate spit up.

**45.** You really hate it when someone else is sicker than you are.

**46.** The sight of a small finger in a nose makes you ill.

**47.** You hate homemade presents, especially Playdough blobs.

**48.** You abhor refrigerator magnets.

**49.** The very thought of little boots, little sneakers, and little sandals all lined up by the door makes you want to scream.

**50.** You hate glue on the computer keyboard.

**51.** Glitter makes you sneeze.

**52.** You dislike chocolate-chip cookies.

**53.** You think sidewalk chalk is messy.

**54.** You hate to walk in the woods.

**55.** You think snow is a curse.

**56.** You hate to read aloud.

**57.** You hate to play Candyland.

**58.** You hate to play Go-Fish.

**59.** You think frogs are gross.

**60.** You hate dirt.

**61.** You hate to build sandcastles.

**62.** You think beaches are for lying on.

**63.** You never want to do homework again.

**64.** You especially never want to do algebra homework again.

**65.** You hate school plays.

**66.** The sound of the letters PTA makes you think of your mother.

**67.** You hate volunteer work.

**68.** You hate to sit and wait.

**69.** You're afraid to set foot in the emergency room or any room in a hospital.

**70.** Runny noses make you gag.

**71.** Ear wax makes you gag.

**72.** You don't think cars should be eaten in.

**73.** You were never any good at school projects.

**74.** You could never be a room parent.

**75.** You never have wanted a pet mouse.

**76.** You hate the way those little electrical outlet plugs look.

**77.** You think a drink means scotch.

**78.** You like to shop alone.

**79.** You hate to go grocery shopping.

**80.** You like to shop in peace.

**81.** You hate arguing in public.

**82.** You mean No the first time you say it.

**83.** Compromise isn't part of your nature.

**84.** You'd like to shoot the ice cream man.

**85.** You hate sand in your car.

**86.** You hate all foreign objects in your car.

**87.** You really can't stand it when people throw up all over your new car.

**88.** You hate the very idea of having to share your car with someone, especially when that someone might be a spacey teenager!

**89.** You can't drive when people are shrieking.

**90.** You hate to read aloud the same thing night after night.

**91.** You don't believe in a little bit of magic.

**92.** You think the tooth fairy is gay.

**93.** You think Santa needs to go on a diet.

**94.** You could never deal with someone else's PMS.

**95.** You would die if someone threw up something pink on the new carpeting.

**96.** Your idea of decorating does not include Golden Books and sticky blocks.

**97.** You hate little socks.

**98.** Stuffed animals raise your glucose level.

**99.** Mr. Rogers gives you seizures.

**100.** You hate to take pictures.

**101.** You hate to take videos.

**102.** You hate to watch home videos.

**103.** You don't like anyone to sit in your lap.

**104.** You never liked making snowflakes out of folded paper.

**105.** You have no idea what a sippy cup is.

**106.** You'd faint if you saw someone else get a shot.

**107.** You could never stick your fingers down someone else's throat to pull out who knows what, even if that person was blue all over.

**108.** You hate whining.

**109.** You have never liked pets.

**110.** You have no patience for procrastination.

**111.** You'd absolutely croak if someone other than the dog ate out of the dog bowl.

**112.** You could never decide between disposables or cloth.

**113.** You don't know who Carmen San Diego is.

**114.** You could never stay awake long enough to pick someone up from a school dance at 10:00 P.M.

**115.** You find it difficult to choose your own clothes, never mind someone else's.

**116.** Ivory Soap snow creations give you a rash.

**117.** You think Raffi is something you swing from.

**118.** Strained peas make your stomach turn.

**119.** You think drool is vile.

**120.** You hate drool in the vegetable dip.

**121.** You want your laces to be in your own shoes.

**122.** You dislike driving.

**123.** You hate driving to the orthodontist.

**124.** You hate driving to the dentist.

**125.** You hate to watch people pull out their own teeth, then wait to get money for them.

**126.** You can't stay up late enough to be transformed into the tooth fairy or Santa.

**127.** You don't want to wait in line to practice the piano.

**128.** You hate soccer.

**129.** You hate football.

**130.** You hate all sports.

**131.** It ticks you off when you find Cheerios in the VCR.

**132.** You want the comics first.

**133.** It would really frost you if today's paper turned into paper doll garlands.

**134.** You just can't understand how anyone could mistake the cat box for a sandbox.

**135.** You would never dream of letting anyone play with cornmeal, in a box, on the kitchen floor.

**136.** You think growing crystals is stupid.

**137.** You don't like those little cupcake papers.

**138.** You can't scrape vomit off of sheets at 3:00 A.M.

**139.** You hate swings.

**140.** You can't ride a bike.

**141.** You're a sound sleeper.

**142.** You can't do hair.

**143.** You could never teach someone to drive.

**144.** You're a terrible teacher.

**145.** You hate to listen to early readers read.

**146.** You never want to be a grandparent.

**147.** You hate tattling.

**148.** You like to watch the 6 o'clock news.

**149.** You want your mother all to yourself.

**150.** You want your spouse all to yourself.

**151.** You love long, uninterrupted baths.

**152.** You love long, hot showers.

**153.** You love geraniums, not airplane swings, on your deck.

**154.** You think snacking is bad for people's health.

**155.** You hate the smell of Cheerios.

**156.** You can't stand girls crying in the bathroom at school dances.

**157.** You hate toothless grins.

**158.** You can't stand having your leg hugged or your shirt pulled.

**159.** You hate getting up in the middle of the night.

**160.** You have no tolerance for other people's nightmares.

**161.** You could never understand how scary the wind can be.

**162.** You have a "stop only once" rule for long car trips.

**163.** You hate grape juice.

**164.** You hate having dependents.

**165.** You like Masterpiece Theater.

**166.** You like Public Radio.

**167.** You hate the smell of Desitin.

**168.** You could never take a rectal temperature.

**169.** You don't do diaper bags.

**170.** You hate scraping clay off the floor.

**171.** You don't enjoy visiting bathrooms every five minutes while you're in strange cities.

**172.** You don't like being beaten at chess.

**173.** You could never understand why anyone would want to get out of bed ten to twelve times each night.

**174.** You hate to see cats carried around by their tails.

**175.** You don't know why the sky is blue.

**176.** You also don't know why the ocean is blue.

**177.** You were never any good with a telescope.

**178.** You have no idea why the moon shines.

**179.** You're not sure where the universe ends.

**180.** You hate orange ice pops.

**181.** You hate homemade ice pops.

**182.** Tootsie Roll lollipops make your teeth ache.

**183.** You don't like sharing licks on pops.

**184.** You have no interest in growing butter-flies or hatching frogs.

**185.** Strained applesauce makes you barf.

**186.** Playing peekaboo at 2:00 A.M. makes you mean.

**187.** You don't like being told you're wrong.

**188.** You hate it when anyone slams the door.

**189.** You hate it when people don't shut the front door.

**190.** You never heard of a Boo-Boo Bunny.

**191.** You can't drive when people are singing "The Wheels on the Bus Go Round and Round" for the one-hundredth time.

**192.** You like your fine-lined markers to stay that way.

**193.** The thought of a college fund makes you nauseous—you haven't paid off your own student loans.

**194.** You dislike pink food.

**195.** You don't want to be responsible for screwing up another person like your parents did you.

**196.** You hate finger paints.

**197.** You can't stand toy catalogs.

**198.** You think it's wasteful to squirt a whole can of shaving cream in the sink.

**199.** You hate teddy bears.

**200.** You'd like to strangle Lamb Chop.

**201.** You hate ripped furniture.

**202.** You hate worn-out rugs.

**203.** Pacifiers make you gag.

**204.** Wet thumbs make you ill.

**205.** You hate Band-Aids.

**206.** You hate pet funerals, especially in the winter.

**207.** You like sharp scissors.

**208.** You hate glue on your scissors.

**209.** You really hate beeswax on your scissors.

**210.** You don't like making dolls' clothes.

**211.** You think the Easter Bunny should grow up.

**212.** You don't like sharing your food.

**213.** You like to keep a secret stash of chocolate in the house.

**214.** You hate hide-and-seek.

**215.** You hate noise!

**216.** You like to talk on the phone without being interrupted.

**217.** You hate being interrupted when you're talking to your spouse.

**218.** You never want to write another compare-and-contrast paper.

**219.** You can't do advanced calculus.

**220.** Calculus hadn't been invented when you went to school.

**221.** You have no idea what a binomial integer is.

**222.** You never want to have anything to do with college applications, ever again!

**223.** You like to see the mail first.

**224.** You hate band instruments.

**225.** You hate having to repeat yourself.

**226.** You have no interest in birds' nests.

**227.** You would never bring a baby bird into the house.

**228.** You hate toy trains.

**229.** You're really bad at putting things together.

**230.** You think Halloween should be abolished.

**231.** You like to nap without worrying about being burned alive.

**232.** You like to nap without worrying about who's finger painting.

**233.** You don't like the sound of plastic toys in the garbage disposal.

**234.** You like dinner to last longer than three minutes and forty-five seconds.

**235.** You hate making birthday cakes.

**236.** You don't know the first thing about baking.

**237.** The thought of twenty two-year-olds destroying your house for a birthday party, sends you to your shrink.

**238.** You like romantic dinners for two.

**239.** You like peace and quiet at the dinner table.

**240.** You'd die if you got pooped on.

**241.** You hate wasting food.

**242.** You like to see every new movie as soon as it comes out.

**243.** You think backpacks are for hiking, not babies.

**244.** Crying babies make you think of shake, rattle, and roll.

**245.** You like that last little piece of cake to be there—for you—later.

**246.** You always have to have the biggest piece of pie or cake.

**247.** Your pantyhose is not meant for puppets.

**248.** You can't sew costumes.

**249.** You like to relax after dinner.

**250.** The sight of blood makes you panic.

**251.** You don't think Dr. Spock makes good late-night reading.

**252.** You think Dr. Spock was on STAR TREK.

**253.** If you ever saw anything green come out of a nose, you'd do a double hurl.

**254.** A picnic means aged fromage on crusty French, not PB&J on Wonder white.

**255.** You can't cope when something breaks.

**256.** You can't draw smiley faces on Band-Aids.

**257.** You can't draw faces on hard-boiled eggs.

**258.** You hate dying Easter eggs.

**259.** Blue frosting makes you gag.

**260.** You only like white frosting.

**261.** You hate gingerbread houses.

**262.** You can't sing "Twinkle, Twinkle, Little Star."

**263.** You hate Mother Goose.

**264.** You think Winnie The Pooh is a poop.

**265.** You think Cock Robin is risqué.

**266.** You don't like the color pink.

**267.** You have a bad temper.

**268.** You hate sprouting carrot tops.

**269.** You don't think mashed potatoes should be sculpted.

**270.** You gag when you see ketchup on mashed potatoes or tofu.

**271.** You hate it when the carrots are pulled before they're two inches long.

**272.** You think everyone should eat with a fork.

**273.** You like to travel with one suitcase, not ten.

**274.** Your idea of a vacation is the two of you at Club Med.

**275.** You'd seethe if you had to cancel plans because of someone else's illness.

**276.** You hate theme parks, Disney World, and roller coasters.

**277.** You don't know what a booster seat is.

**278.** You would never drive back sixty miles to retrieve someone's blankie from a rest stop.

**279.** You hate finding tape on the computer screen, the floor, and your pencils.

**280.** You like pencils with points.

**281.** You like to have at least one pen in the house.

**282.** You want NEWSWEEK and THE NEW YORKER, not HUMPTY DUMPTY and TEEN.

**283.** You never liked "99 Bottles of Beer on the Wall."

**284.** You think all teenagers smell bad.

**285.** You never want to get a call from the school principal.

**286.** You never want to get a call from the school telling you your kid threw up on the bus.

**287.** You don't want to spend your Saturdays doing bottle drives.

**288.** Science fairs make you cringe.

**289.** You have no idea how to research summer camps.

**290.** You don't want to drive a "snowflake" to play rehearsals.

**291.** You hate being called mean, unfair, weird, and dweeby.

**292.** You hate planting green-bean seeds in yogurt containers in February.

**293.** You hate wet kisses.

**294.** You have no idea how to make a croup tent.

**295.** You never heard of Ring Dings and Ding Dongs.

**296.** You can't understand how someone could get to the top of a ski slope and refuse to go down.

**297.** You hate car pools.

**298.** You don't think tulips are for picking.

**299.** You hate wilted bouquets.

**300.** You would never keep a stray dog.

**301.** You don't think much of chocolate pudding finger paints on the kitchen table.

**302.** You can't understand why, if the food gets mixed up in the mouth and stomach, it can't touch on the plate.

**303.** You think children should be banned from airplanes.

**304.** You think sleepovers should be outlawed.

**305.** You hate fighting.

**306.** You love to wear cashmere sweaters at home.

**307.** It drives you nuts when people won't try new foods.

**308.** You hate it when you can't find the portable phone because it's in someone's bed.

**309.** You like to travel light.

**310.** You can't remember your car keys, much less the crackers, juice, and activity books.

**311.** You hate playing "Name That State" in the car.

**312.** Posters taped to your nineteenth-century reproduction wallpaper cause you to stop breathing.

**313.** You seethe at fingerprints on the windows.

**314.** You don't think Jack Frost's designs are special.

**315.** You think shaving cream fights should be outlawed.

**316.** You hate little heart-shaped peanut butter sandwiches.

**317.** You don't think anyone under twelve should be allowed to eat ice cream cones.

**318.** You don't own any cookie cutters.

**319.** You hate cookie cutters.

**320.** You think tricycles are only for outside.

**321.** You hate scratched floors.

**322.** You hate the Brothers' Grimm.

**323.** You never read C. S. Lewis.

**324.** Patty-cake makes you sick.

**325.** You would squash the eensy-weensy spider and throw him away in a tissue.

**326.** You hate love notes.

**327.** You hate receiving homemade valentines.

**328.** You hate making homemade valentines.

**329.** You don't like being called at work.

**330.** You hate skin rashes.

**331.** You require a lot of attention.

**332.** You think "Good Night Moon" is a song by Frank Sinatra.

**333.** You wish Farmer McGregor had eaten Peter Rabbit for his supper.

**334.** You hate tea parties.

**335.** You hate it when people jump into a pile
of leaves you just finished raking.

**336.** You can't skip stones.

**337.** You hate catching minnows in nets.

**338.** You don't like being paddled around in circles in your canoe.

**339.** You never liked collecting shells or shiny stones.

**340.** You hate playing catch.

**341.** You think Sundays are for relaxing with coffee and the paper.

**342.** You don't like picking scrambled eggs out of the carpet.

**343.** You value your antique bottle collection more than life itself.

**344.** You hate it when you discover sand on the kitchen floor.

**345.** You hate computer games.

**346.** You could never brush someone else's teeth.

**347.** You could never floss someone else's teeth.

**348.** You never liked carrying around little Tupperware containers of Cheerios.

**349.** You hate Tupperware.

**350.** Mary Poppins sends you into a diabetic coma.

**351.** You don't know how to build a Lincoln Log house.

**352.** You can't build a Lego castle.

**353.** You don't know the difference between Duplos and Legos.

**354.** You have no desire for a horse in your garage.

**355.** You don't want one hundred Matchbox cars parked in front of your couch.

**356.** You dislike discussing the passing of gas at the dinner table.

**357.** You dislike discussing bodily functions at the table.

**358.** You especially dislike discussing other people's bodily functions at the table.

**359.** You hate bathroom jokes.

**360.** You could never deal with head lice.

**361.** You don't like wet people crawling into your bed at 3:00 A.M.

**362.** You hate the smell of pee.

**363.** You hate bathrooms that smell like pee.

**364.** You like the toilet seat down.

**365.** You could never teach someone how to target shoot into the toilet (although it beats pee all over the walls and floor).

**366.** You hate it when people squeeze the toothpaste from the middle.

**367.** You could never be the proud owner of a minivan with an integrated child seat, whatever that is.

**368.** You don't have the patience to teach someone how to play chess.

**369.** You never want to search under beds for little socks.

**370.** You have no idea how to install or use childproof latches on cabinets.

**371.** You hate it when people say, "You never..."

**372.** You hate scraping silly putty off the oriental rug.

**373.** You weren't a psychology major.

**374.** You don't think seaweed hair is elegant.

**375.** You always give your old dress-up clothes to charity.

**376.** You take it personally when people juggle in the house.

**377.** You hate taking people shopping with you who juggle the fruit in the grocery store.

**378.** You hate having your books scribbled on.

**379.** You have no idea how to use a glue gun.

**380.** You never did learn how to knit or sew.

**381.** You don't enjoy bringing people glasses of water in the middle of the night.

**382.** You never enjoyed changing wet sheets two or three times in the middle of the night.

**383.** You never liked sleeping in a wet twin bed, with a small wet person.

**384.** You don't want your bathroom floor coated with a layer of baby powder.

**385.** You've never tried to feed a bird out of your hand.

**386.** You can't remember to call your mother, much less take a baby with you.

**387.** You can't deal with house sitters, let alone babysitters.

**388.** You don't want a basketball hoop in your driveway.

**389.** You'd be ill if someone spilled grape juice on your new sofa.

**390.** You don't like your fall bulbs planted upside down.

**391.** You wouldn't like being told at 10:00 P.M. that a school project on the Byzantine Empire was due the next day.

**392.** Even the idea of being drooled on makes you ill.

**393.** You could never shave someone else's armpits.

**394.** You hate stickers on your furniture.

**395.** You don't think bunny dishes are cute.

**396.** You hate to pick apples.

**397.** You don't care how they make maple syrup.

**398.** You haven't heard of Laura Ingalls Wilder.

**399.** You can't make a snowperson.

**400.** You hate snowball fights.

**401.** You hate carving pumpkins.

**402.** You hate the way pumpkin pulp looks as it's squished through pudgy little fingers.

**403.** You hate wiping up slimy pumpkin pulp and picking the seeds out of the rug.

**404.** You never could carve a pumpkin without slicing off the teeth.

**405.** You still can't light a candle in a pumpkin.

**406.** You don't know how to toast pumpkin seeds.

**407.** You don't know what glitter glue is.

**408.** You can't cut bats out of black construction paper.

**409.** Construction paper makes you sneeze.

**410.** You never want to keep crickets in a little cage on the windowsill.

**411.** You never heard of a B.R.A.T. diet.

**412.** You hate rice on the floor.

**413.** You've never heard of a training bra.

**414.** You don't think magnets are interesting.

**415.** You think icicles are too dirty to eat.

**416.** You think all stray cats have rabies.

**417.** You thought chickenpox had been eradicated along with smallpox.

**418.** You had no idea that chickenpox could be painful.

**419.** You also thought scarlet fever was a thing of the past.

**420.** Coughing children drive you crazy.

**421.** You had no idea a child could cough for a month.

**422.** You don't know how to make a snow angel.

**423.** You have no use for stickers.

**424.** You hate to worry.

**425.** You don't know how to use mitten clips.

**426.** You don't like G-rated movies.

**427.** You're just a grumpy old curmudgeon.

**428.** You think homemade holiday door decorations are ugly.

**429.** You couldn't deal with a person who sleeps with a stuffed tiger, yet wants to go out on dates.

**430.** You couldn't show someone how to knit two hundred times.

**431.** You don't want to live with someone who might point a finger at you and go "Pow, pow!"

**432.** You never want to rescue someone from the top of a tree.

**433.** You don't know how to make a blanket fort.

**434.** You don't find airplanes exciting when they're sitting on the ground.

**435.** You don't think bats are cute.

**436.** You have no use for two thousand empty baby-food jars.

**437.** You would never loan a scarf to a snow-man.

**438.** You're into power walking, not picking rabbit's-foot clover.

**439.** You have no idea what rabbit's-foot clover is.

**440.** You have a tendency to rake up all leaf houses.

**441.** You hate little plastic dishes.

**442.** Cute little music boxes that play "It's a Small World" over and over drive you nuts.

**443.** Writing in the fog on the bathroom mirror drives you crazy.

**444.** You think potatoes are for eating, not turning into people heads.

**445.** You do not want pictures of stick figures standing outside of tilted houses to grace your refrigerator.

**446.** You do not want anybody telling anyone what you look like in the morning.

**447.** You do not like tiny, muddy boot prints on the car dashboard.

**448.** Melted Lifesavers on the car seats drive you bonkers.

**449.** You can't understand why anyone would unroll an entire roll of toilet paper just to see how long it is.

**450.** You can't understand why anyone would give the toilet paper holder a good spin, over and over and over.

**451.** It really drives you nuts when someone twenty years younger than you is better at the computer than you.

**452.** You could never sit up all night in a hospital room with a small person who is sick after a tonsillectomy.

**453.** You couldn't concentrate enough to drive a small screaming person with a broken arm to the emergency room.

**454.** You've never heard of impetigo.

**455.** You don't think sticks should be turned into swords or guns.

**456.** You don't have the patience to pitch two thousand balls to someone who misses every time.

**457.** You couldn't tell someone they did a good job after missing two thousand pitches.

**458.** Your back hurts too much to run alongside a little bicycle a hundred times yelling, "Good, good. You've got it."

**459.** You have no idea how to put on training wheels.

**460.** Broken bones make you faint.

**461.** Split lips gushing blood also make you faint.

**462.** Bloody noses in the car cause you to have accidents.

**463.** You don't think fast-food meals should come with toys.

**464.** You find hiking with someone who refuses to pee in the woods really annoying.

**465.** You'd like to have nice furniture before you're fifty.

**466.** You'd like to refinish the floors before you're fifty.

**467.** You think the $125,000 you'll spend per child for college would be better spent on a sailboat.

**468.** You think children's literature is what authors wrote while working their way up to adult literature.

**469.** You're still changing careers. How could you counsel anyone on career goals?

**470.** You don't like all your shampoo and conditioner used to make concoctions.

**471.** You don't know how to pretend to eat a soap-bubble cake.

**472.** You don't know that glycerin is what makes really cool big bubbles.

**473.** You thought tie-dye went out in the sixties.

**474.** You don't find flashlights amusing.

**475.** You would never gunk up a ceiling with glow-in-the-dark stars and constellations.

**476.** You have no imagination.

**477.** You hate the noise of Slinkies going down the stairs.

**478.** You could never eat with a retainer on the table or floating in a glass of water.

**479.** You have no interest in spending $3,000 to straighten teeth, only to have them knocked out with a field hockey stick.

**480.** You think large cardboard cartons should be recycled, not made into clubhouses.

**481.** You think tree houses look awful.

**482.** You would never sit in a tree house for a secret club meeting.

**483.** You would not like having $200 worth of groceries consumed in one afternoon by a hoard of hungry teenagers.

**484.** You don't know what a macaroni picture is.

**485.** You would vacuum up a card path and eat the treasure at the end of it.

**486.** You can't think of clues for treasure hunts.

**487.** You can't make newspaper hats.

**488.** You could never tolerate paper chains on your Christmas tree.

**489.** You never could put together those balsa-wood airplanes.

**490.** You couldn't make a paper airplane to save your life.

**491.** You hate kites.

**492.** You don't know how to make relief maps with clay.

**493.** Inside-out eyelids make you sick.

**494.** You don't understand why everyone can't float the first time they try.

**495.** You'll never understand why someone still can't dive after a hundred lessons.

**496.** You wouldn't be caught dead skiing on the bunny hill with a rope attached to a small snow bunny in front of you.

**497.** You don't have the patience to ski with a small, slippery, nylon, poufy bundle between your legs whose skis keep scratching yours.

**498.** You can't understand how anyone could fall off a chairlift.

**499.** You'll never understand how someone could drop their gloves and one ski pole from a chairlift.

**500.** You have no clue as to how someone could lose their winter jacket every other day.

**501.** You just might strangle someone who lost all their books on the second day of seventh grade.

**502.** You couldn't understand how someone could leave their backpack with a lunch inside in another state while at a concert.

**503.** You couldn't deal with the backpack that was returned after two weeks that had been left in another state with the lunch inside.

**504.** You have no idea how boys' jockstraps are sized.

**505.** You don't know that children can get migraine headaches.

**506.** Your idea of fun isn't making a luge trail on the hill behind your house.

**507.** You freeze just thinking about teaching a three-foot-tall person how to ice skate.

**508.** You hate picking wildflowers and making daisy chains.

**509.** You think pressing flowers is a waste of time.

**510.** The words "gee goo ga ga" could never come out of your mouth.

**511.** You do not think people should sit under the table in restaurants.

**512.** You think marbles are what your Aunt Agnes lost several years ago.

**513.** You don't know how to iron crayons and autumn leaves into waxed paper.

**514.** You think mud belongs outside, not tracked all over your floors.

**515.** You hate getting your socks wet because a small person got snow plops all over the floor.

**516.** You don't know how to grow wheat grass in baskets for Easter.

**517.** You hate fireworks.

**518.** You couldn't understand why someone would be too frightened to step over a dead moth.

**519.** You would never allow grape juice in your house.

**520.** You've never made Rice Krispy treats.

**521.** You hate the sight of marigolds coming up over the sides of cottage cheese containers in March.

**522.** You would have trouble restraining yourself if someone said that the beach was boring after spending two hours getting there.

**523.** You don't know that a sick, vomiting child can generate fifty loads of laundry in three days.

**524.** You believe you have enough linens to take care of a vomiting child.

**525.** You don't know just how many ear infections one child can have in a year.

**526.** You'd die if you had to ride in a hotel elevator with a small, blue-lipped, dripping-wet person wearing fins, a face mask, and snorkel.

**527.** You hate dead goldfish.

**528.** You don't want an iguana living in your kitchen.

**529.** You never want to know the pattern of your pediatrician's waiting room rug better than the back of your own hand.

**530.** You'd rather not choose a hotel just because it has a pool.

**531.** You don't have the patience to set up a thousand-piece domino race course.

**532.** You don't know what a domino race course is.

**533.** You have no idea what wipes are.

**534.** You only own one tote bag.

**535.** Your hallway was not meant as a keeper of bats, gloves, smelly shoes, and balls.

**536.** You'll never understand baby clothes sized in months.

**537.** You don't know how to make a diorama.

**538.** You could never wriggle a squiggly person into a footed sleeper.

**539.** You don't know how to cook one-handed with a baby slung on your hip.

**540.** You never want to cook wearing a baby in a backpack.

**541.** You don't find evening wear attractive with a snugly in the front.

**542.** You hate to feed ducks.

**543.** You hate petting zoos.

**544.** You couldn't imagine anyone opening your home-office door without knocking.

**545.** You do not see the joy in remote-control cars.

**546.** When the phone rings, you want it to be for you.

**547.** You don't want to ever have to worry about someone else getting pregnant.

**548.** Baby toes make you sick.

**549.** You agree with your mother that cotton candy should be outlawed.

**550.** You'll never understand how someone could lose three new watches in one month.

**551.** You couldn't tolerate one small person slugging another small person in the arm every time they passed each other.

**552.** You couldn't understand the words "nothing to do" with two thousand toys and books in the house.

**553.** You don't like people looking through your drawers.

**554.** You don't make homemade doughnuts every fall.

**555.** You can't make a replica of your house out of gingerbread, complete with dormers.

**556.** You don't know that teenagers still like to lie on their parents' bed at night.

**557.** You don't know that the best conversations with teenagers start late at night.

**558.** You don't think people should have purple or orange elastic on their braces.

**559.** You don't want to type someone's paper on medieval and early renaissance medicine at 2:00 A.M.

**560.** You'd rather read a novel than quiz someone on organic chemistry.

**561.** You don't think it's cute to have skunks on the deck eating the cat food.

**562.** You find nothing fascinating about watching the water go down the drain in the tub.

**563.** You couldn't understand how anyone could think they might go down the tub drain.

**564.** The first robin of spring doesn't excite you.

**565.** You could never have a pencil holder on your desk that was made from a tin can with multicolored yarn wrapped around it.

**566.** You have no idea what a butterfly bandage is.

**567.** You can't understand how anyone could be afraid of the water.

**568.** You don't think homemade confetti should be thrown on New Year's Eve.

**569.** You like to listen to the news at 7:00 A.M.

**570.** Television shows with puppets on at 7:00 A.M. make you nauseous.

**571.** You are adamant that if you spend $3,000 on summer camp, the camper had better love it.

**572.** You can't understand how someone could be homesick after two hours.

**573.** You have no tolerance for people who don't love mushrooms.

**574.** You don't think there's anything fascinating about cornstarch and water paste.

**575.** You have no tolerance whatsoever for beginning musicians.

**576.** You don't know that some people think they're supposed to kick the soccer ball into their own goal.

**577.** You have no idea that some people are afraid of balls, soccer and otherwise.

**578.** You think babies sleep all night after three weeks.

**579.** You also think babies take four-hour naps every morning and afternoon.

**580.** You don't know that babies aren't content to look at mobiles for more than thirty seconds.

**581.** You don't know that it will be twelve years before you can leave a child home alone so you don't have to arrange for a babysitter.

**582.** You haven't a clue that some people think old black-and-white movies are the pits.

**583.** You don't have the patience to travel on a plane with a child who has ear pain.

**584.** You don't know that it sometimes takes as many as three adults to buy shoes for one very small, reluctant person.

**585.** You never learned that some people think if you cut off Barbie's beautiful, long, blonde hair, it will grow back.

**586.** You never want naked Barbies and Kens in your house.

**587.** You could never put eye drops in a moving target.

**588.** You think disappearing eyeballs are scary.

**589.** You despise rubber insects and snakes.

**590.** You don't do gingerbread houses.

**591.** You have no idea how to make a cottage cheese face.

**592.** You don't think beds resemble trampolines.

**593.** You're frightened of headless dolls.

**594.** You never want rusty, yellow, metal trucks on your lawn.

**595.** You don't want a real live duck living in a blue plastic wading pool on your deck.

**596.** You don't want to feel guilty every time you go out to dinner and a movie.

**597.** You want to see a movie that isn't animated when you do go out.

**598.** You enjoy looking at art in museums, not visiting the bathrooms.

**599.** You find nothing amusing about electric-eye toilets or sinks.

**600.** You enjoy living alone in your sterile, petless apartment, listening to opera while dining on French wine and cheese.

## How to score the Parental Aptitude Test

Okay, so let's see how you did.

For every D answer, give yourself 25 points.
For every C, give yourself 15 points.
For every B, subtract 5 points.
For every A, subtract 10 points.

If you scored a perfect 425 points, you are truly an excellent candidate for parenthood or are a perfect parent.

255-420: you'll be okay as a parent, but you'll need some work.

Less than 150: you're an uptight piece of work and should never, never have kids, lest you raise them to be the boring, unspontaneous person you are.

ISBN 1-888952-31-8

6  10529 00038  4